ABOUT THE AUTHOR

Neelam Saredia-Brayley is an award-winning poet, captivating audiences for the past decade. Effortlessly warm and honest, Neelam works with illustrators, musicians and dancers, creating unique, multi-disciplinary performances.

Neelam has headlined and performed at events across the UK including Apples and Snake's 451 City, Hammer and Tongue, Sofar Sounds Cambridge, Jawdance, Greenbelt Festival, Possible's Climate Cabaret, and at Turner Contemporary. She has appeared on BBC Radio Kent, BBC Upload Festival and CSRfm.

In 2019 she received Arts Council funding to develop her project, 'Queer Brown Skin'. In 2020 Neelam was awarded the Apples and Snakes: Jerwood Arts | Poetry in Performance Award. Neelam has been commissioned by National Poetry Day 2021, and was selected for Midwest Video Poetry Fest 2021 as well as the New York International Arts Festival 2021.

Neelam reaches out to the daughters of immigrants; to mothers who stay; to girls who love girls; to girls who sing hurricanes away.

She lives in Kent with her husband and creative partner, Adrian (who also illustrated this book cover).

Faecbook: Neelam Saredia-Brayley Poetry
Instagram: neelam_the_poet
Twitter: @neelam_saredia

PRAISE FOR NEELAM:

'Utterly compelling...her poetry is emotive and humorous, full of rhythmic and tonal surprises. She is one to watch.'
- Lydia McCutcheon, Canterbury Culture

'Her work is always striking, thoughtful, innovative and plural.'
- Joelle Taylor, Poet, Playwright, Author & Founder of SLAMbassadors, TS Eliot Prize winner

'Her voice is exactly what power in protest and the power of women is about.'
- Power of Women Festival

Neelam Saredia-Brayley
RANI

VERVE
POETRY PRESS
BIRMINGHAM

PUBLISHED BY VERVE POETRY PRESS
https://vervepoetrypress.com
mail@vervepoetrypress.com

All rights reserved
© 2022 Neelam Saredia-Brayley
The right of Neelam Saredia-Brayley to be identified as author of this work has been asserted in accordance with section 77 of the Copyright, Designs and Patents Act 1988.

No part of this work may be reproduced, stored or transmitted in any form or by any means, graphic, electronic, recorded or mechanical, without the prior written permission of the publisher.

FIRST PUBLISHED OCT 2022

Printed and bound in the UK
by ImprintDigital, Exeter

ISBN: 978-1-913917-17-3

For my beautiful, glorious, resilient family.

For my husband Adrian, my reason for carrying on and always having hope.

*And for you, survivors.
You are meant to be here.*

CONTENTS

One - And We Held Sunlight in Our Palms

Glory Days	13
Southall	15
Summers	18
Growing	20

Two - The Trauma Bones of Quiet Daughters

Swimming	25
The Waiting Room	28
Airport Security	30
Thirds	33
Correction	35
Differences	36
Posing for Photos to Put in My 'If I Go Missing' Folder	38
Lost Property	41
Faces	43

Three - Planting Wildflowers

Wives	47
Dandelions	49
Bruises	50
August	52
Hope is Like Being Haunted	54
Blessing	56

Four - Fragments: Stories from the Other Side

Silverware	59
There's No Time Like the Pandemic	61
Deer Watching	62
Migration	63
Union	66
Sand Timer	68
You Tell Me You're an Organ Donor	69
'Upholding the Law Fairly and Firmly'	71
La Vie En Rose	72
Transformation	75

Five - How to Turn Your Body into a Forest Fire

Regenerating	79
Women of the Sea	81
Poetry of Resistance	83
Art Lessons	86
Rani Lakshmibai of Jhansi	87
Body	92

Glossary
Acknowledgements

RANI

One:
And We Held Sunlight in Our Palms

Glory Days

On the best days
our bicycles were chariots.

We rode in V-formation
a flock of children
taking turns being the leader
riding all the way to glory.

We hummed, a heartbeat of pedals
spurs glinting in the sunlight
sent smiles scattering through alleyways
left them shooting up through the guttering
like fireworks.

Dad took the stabilisers off
only needed to hold the seat once
for me to pick up two-wheel cycling.

I crashed into a parked van later
but it didn't stop me.

We cycled up the sides of school buildings
only to feel a fresher air on our skin
planted flags with our tyres.

We were invincible
as long as we were back at the dinner table by six.

We piled up at the kitchen door
with plates full

hands washed
but forearms and backs of necks
still holding sunlight
that *outside* smell
we went to bed with it
always wanting to sleep out in the garden
but never quite being brave enough
to last the whole night.

But each day we went further
seeing how far we could make it before curfew.

We revved our rubber handles
three little Evel Knievels
gliding
sure-footed
even in the air
pitching laughs across canyons of concrete.

Now, I've grown.
I return to the garage.

Our bikes are so small
they collect dust
and echoes.

The bells have ginger rust spots
the ring sounds crunchy and dull.

But I find glory can still be seen
from the front door

shining bright
in infinite
victory.

Southall

I grew up in Southall
if people haven't heard of it
I say *about half an hour away from Heathrow airport.*

We measure distances by how close we come to flying.

In Southall, the signs are written in English and Punjabi.
Down the Broadway
you can smell sweet orange jalebi being fried in vats of oil
packed into boxes from family hands
to family hands
children clustering around the stalls
the syrup leaking from the corner of the paper bag
on the car ride home.

The musky suits from India
are lifted gently like precious paintings
rolls of dyed cotton
spread out over market stalls
peacock blues, emeralds, burgundy.

The hopefulness of beauty parlours
the melting wax, double twine threading
eyebrows and upper lip in under five minutes
talcum powder and incense
hallowed places to strip away stubborn hair
leave humbled, sore and reborn.

Walk past jewellery shops
selling yellow gold in red cushioned boxes
hundreds of wedding rings that come in pairs.

In the fruit and veg shop next door
the lilt of 126 red bangles
as three recent brides quickly pick the best green chillies
from a mountain of them in yellow crates.
These wedding chura used to be ivory
now layers of plastic
but still a symbol of fortune, fertility, prosperity
expected to stay on for a month and a quarter
or until they snap off naturally
the remains falling on who might marry next.

Gurdwaras in white marble and gold domes
streetlights for the walk home
the Himalayan cinema that only shows Hindi movies
red buses on the Broadway
winding round blocks of flats and temples
reaching my grandparents' house.

Their garden full of tomatoes
strawberries and raspberries ready for plucking
drying bunches of methi in the sun
wrapped up in an old peach chunni.
The musty garage that dried out throats
if you stayed there too long
the wooden rocking horse
with stuck-on eyes and white mop hair
a stationary, permanent resident.

I miss the cash and carry shops
with packs of atta stacked from floor to head-height
vegetables I didn't know the words for in English
like arbi
and ended up saying
it's like a potato
but with the hair and skin of a coconut
but it's potatoey inside?

I remember being allergic to its skin
getting a red rash from palms to fingertips
after peeling arbi the way grownups do
prickling skin growing to a rising burn
by the evening.

Gingerly
I spread aloe vera gel between my hands
listened to planes rumbling overhead
from Heathrow to the horizon.

The Hondas drove past in the drizzle,
each one like long sighs on the asphalt
accompanied by the thumping bass of Punjabi bhangra.
I fell asleep with my palms up
like a surrender.

Summers

The hours were filled with
daring each other to eat handfuls of lemon slices
or smell old jars of mustard

elbowing each other under the table
whilst keeping a completely straight face

bubblegum ice cream secretly before lunch
but not being able to hide the blue corners of our mouths.

We wore baggy t-shirts tucked into shorts
that fell below the knees
that used to be jogging bottoms.

And often the wrong clothes to the beach
always coming home with pants full of sand.
Some rinsed down the plughole
but most sprinkled in our beds overnight.

We played on the swings at Nana and Nani's house
with our eyes closed
until we saw pink shapes behind our eyelids
they looked like heaven.

I see this in neon
the exhilaration
endless tomorrows
and summers that always managed to stretch out before us.

I imagine a pink halo over these years
it fits just right.

I take a picture with my eyes
hold it until the glow fades.

Growing

Do you remember when you were in Year 1
and you had a peg with your own name on it?

It was an anchor
a lighthouse
just for you.

It kept your place
a bookmark
and you knew you belonged.

You'd carefully hang up your rocket backpack
and puffy coat
the one with mittens sewn on the sleeves
with a piece of elastic so you didn't lose them
but that didn't stop you from accidentally dipping them
in every puddle across the playground.

But the silver peg
so kind and sturdy
would help them dry by home time.

It was hard to switch to a new peg in September
but it was unavoidable.

Before summer, you collected your coat
your paint-stained jumper
your bookbag with half-peeled Velcro
the P.E. shorts you thought you lost
at the beginning of term

and moved on.

It took a small period of adjustment
sometimes forgetting and shuffling back to the old peg
but finding someone else's name on it
and bundled with coats that weren't yours.

Over time
you got used to it.
Your new peg was closer to your class
and it learnt how to hold your most precious things
just as well.

It was your first lesson in accepting change
in learning to let go.

Two: The Trauma Bones of Quiet Daughters

Swimming

When I was eleven, swimming lessons were mandatory.

Each week
clothes nervously shedding
gangly limbs and sucked-in stomach rolls
the sound of a swimming cap
smacking around someone's skull.
Hearing screams
making sure they weren't coming out of my mouth
without me noticing.

Lining up at the deep end
the instructor blowing quicksilver whistles
watching others jump

not diving in

eventually
sitting at the cold edge
lowering
slowly crumpling
to the pool floor.

Gruelling minutes later
I half-starfished in the shallows.
The instructor tipped my chin up
with my nose in the air so I could breathe.

His hands were big and wrinkly
and I felt like I could finally float.

But the moment his guiding palms left
I capsized under the surface
body of stone
water clogging my nose and throat
chlorine and someone's rogue plaster.

In the almost-drown
I kicked the side of the pool
gripped the ladder
while a strong hand between my shoulder blades
propped me upright
chest realising
it was level with the frothy water.

My lip wobbled.

Patience and warmth radiated
from the instructor's round face
all the way from the top of his glossy bald head
to his stubbly dimpled chin.

I coughed over his words
You'll get it next time.

Behind flimsy blue cubicle curtains
I wrung the sadness out of my costume
telling myself
You only have six minutes to cry
four to pull it back together.

On the coach afterwards
I hoped people believed my red eyes
were from bleach instead of weakness.

There was no determination for next time
just the relief
of coming home
undrowned.

The Waiting Room

There's a half molar wriggling its way out of my mouth.

Tongue-toying
pushing it loose
not quite letting go.

The magazines are from 2014
water stains over faces
the pages crinkle.

The air is tightened
with formocreasol
    cresatin
    clove oil
    acrylic monomer
names repeated to keep calm.

There are framed posters on the walls
with giant static grins
    white teeth
    white skin
    always
a dimple in the corners of lips
a secret we don't share.

Clipboards with green medical forms
the awkwardness of shuffling
of trying not to look at each other
of drilling from down the corridor
we're pretending not to notice.

Pretending so hard
I almost don't hear
the sound of my name
being mispronounced.

Airport Security

Before you get to security
you stand in lines
grey seatbelt borders pulled tight
but there is nothing safe about this.

Bodies in front and behind
the sharp tang of nervous sweat
a conveyor belt of shuffling feet
pulled unwillingly forward.

Taking your shoes off
like you're in a Gurdwara
Mandir
family houses
but there is nothing holy about this.

The hairs of the nylon carpet
nettle up through your socks
and you find yourself starting to pray
please let me make it through.

You remove your jacket
unclasp silver earrings and your belt buckle
the goosebumps rushing to cover exposed skin.
You pull black Kirby grips from your head
they catch four long strands of hair in their mouths.

You place them in the plastic grey tray
thinking if you died unexpectedly
this is what your personal effects box would look like.

This is what they'd hand over to your family
with distant eyes already on the next case.
This is what would be left.

You hand the contents of your body up
to be swallowed whole on the conveyer belt
an unarmed *please don't shoot.*

The beeps
yes or no
girl or bomb
or both?

You never make it through first time.

Blue gloved hands rolled on slowly
thicker lines of prophylactic plastic at the cuffs
the latex leaving white powder on palms and fingertips
tightening fingers into fists without knowing it.

Boxers' chalk just before a punch.
Your stomach is soft and moth-eaten.

They unpeel the clear plastic bag with your 100ml liquids in
you pick the items of least value to lose
but it's not enough.

They begin to strip-search
pulling skin taut under UV light
finding all the freckles and stretch-marks in hidden places
shoving legs through the gaps of metal hangers
hanging dark-skinned bodies
in the closets of government officials.

Some are never returned.

But you are one of the lucky ones.
You put it back on afterwards.

It doesn't ever fit right.

Thirds

monsoon steam
armfuls of rain
dripping beads
off the corner of a lilac sari
strands of hair
pasted onto creased forehead

wet mangos
in a blue plastic bag
strung over elbow crook

waiting

on street corners

to barter blessings
through exchange of rupees

waiting

for cars to slow
                    one does
window rolls down
thickened hand leaning out
knuckle hair
splattered quickly
with bullets of rain
chooses body
over blessings

kohl smudges
roughly

he drives away

green mangoes
still on the back seat

Correction

There was a mistake
in the way she was born
so
her uncle saw to that.

Differences

In Catholic sixth form
I was christened *terrorist* in my first week.

Terrorist
shouted over shoulders
through blonde curtains
provoked by the darkness of my skin
    the unfamiliarity
    an excuse
    an invitation of arrows
    on my black-and-brown dartboard.

In the Church next door
I carried the body of low-fat Jesus
dripping paraffin candles
and a heavy wooden cross
    delicious dark walnut which I wanted to lick
    but I worried it would neatly tuck long splinters
    on the topside of my tongue
    so resisted temptation.

A token brown girl
on a special mission
to be transformed
    made new
    washed clean.

But Jesus was a brown man too
               Middle Eastern Jew.

On the other side
maybe we can share a cup of cha
with cardamom
    cloves
      an inch of ginger
discuss strategies for lying low at the airport.

Maybe he'll teach me Aramaic
see which Punjabi words sound the same

and we can laugh
at all the differences.

Posing for Photos to Put in My 'If I Go Missing' Folder

1.

God
I hope I look hot in these.
I'll make sure it won't be a blurry newspaper photo
that people have to squint to make out.
It'll be high def as hell
especially if lots of people are looking at it
photocopying
posting
shuffling
dealing.

I want every freckle clearly visible
the constellation of my face
a map
and you better come find me.

It took four hours to write all the information
in that editable saveable PDF.

Eye Colour: brown
Hair Colour: dark brown/black
Tattoos: none
Everyday Jewellery: gold wedding ring
Any Other Identifying Features: small and curvy stature
(5ft 2 – despite outward appearance, I have grown).

Notes on Mental, Emotional and Physical Health
with only two lines of space.
After three tries
the text became very small.

Fingerprints:

Thumb   Index   Middle   Ring   Pinkie

(I used my alphabet stamps' ink for this -
leftover from Valentine's cards).

Work Route
Where Do You Park
Bank Details
Social Media Passwords
Mother Father Sister Brother
Partners
Close Friends
Exes (room for thirteen lucky people).
Previous Addresses
Reasons For Leaving
(do I mention the mould and weed and noise and damp
or do I keep it positive
like it's a job application
a credit reference
to prove I was good and professional at all times).
Frequently Visited Locations
(this becomes harder
whilst living through a pandemic).

Are these photos any good?
Should I suck in a bit more
or show my natural stomach?

(In trauma I might be smaller?)

Do they do me justice?
I swipe through them
tilt my head to the left
big wide smile
I am in my prime (I hope)
a young woman
promising so much
being promised
that I will be found

because I filled in all the paperwork.
I did everything right.

Right?

2.

I know what it's like
to be waiting for a phone call
for any and all news
but being denied information
berated for not having all the details
for not spell-checking in a crisis
for not writing it out Legibly in Black Ink, Bold Capitals.

I did the paperwork for you, love

(you can wait on the sofa with this file in your hands).

Lost Property

Greet your body.

Pick it up from where they finished playing with it
        dropped it from their mouths
        on the cold floor.

Face down
the limbs are stiff
and crossed in careless ways.

You walk quietly beside it
kneel down
put a shaking hand on the back
turn it over
gently
a half-recovery position.

Long hair covers its face
like pulled-up patches of grass
        tied knots
        chewed edges
you smooth it back slowly.

The eyes are still open.

You straighten the limbs
button the blouse back up
pull the jeans up from around the ankles
brush the boot marks off the waistband
bend over the body

and lift.

You carry it away slowly.

It is both heavier
and lighter
than expected.

You give it back your voice box
expect her to start screaming.

She says nothing
neither do you.

Faces

When ticking watch faces are broken by a fall
it tells the time of death
capturing the moment the light went out.

Women's faces
do this too.

Three:
Planting Wildflowers

Wives

They sit cross-legged
on rope-threaded manjas
gossiping
instructing
praying

hands kneading white chapatti flour
peeling red carrots and freckled potatoes
ginger, garlic, green onions
pause only to place sliding chunnis
back around their shoulders.

They stand over hot stoves
bull-strong and resilient
making roti with burning wrists
carrying the sixth pile of clothes upstairs
folding them carefully into drawers
heading back down
for the seventh.

They spend all day anticipating the needs
of their husbands
sons
uncles
cousins
colleagues
fulfilling them silently
in the corners of rooms
the edges of conversations.

They finish cleaning in the quiet dark
careful not to disturb the soft snores
last to bed
first up again tomorrow.

Ex-daughters and sisters
growing up
stepping into marriages
before their time
cementing duty
in seven walks
around the fire.

Wives with stretch marks
and strong arms
the weight of bearing children
soldier on
like fistfuls of coins.

One day
they will melt their dowries
turn it into weaponry

guild their own names.

Dandelions

Dandelions are hardy plants
that green-fingered gardeners pull out
with trowels
hands
forks
and in some cases, poison.

Beloved of grazing animals
they grow in pavement gaps
the spaces between bricks
turning grey with worry
losing their mind over their children
blowing them across the ocean
hoping the water is steady
purposeful
and above all, kind.

Dandelion days are short.

They are uprooted from warm gardens
but find homes in the backyards of the unloved.
Or the fronts of grey flats
that the council pays no one to look after.
There, they survive
they blossom
turning concrete into wildness.

Bruises

Prize boxer-boy
gets goosebumps
from brushing his teeth.

Wipes his mouth on skin
backs of red hands
reverberation from knuckle to nail.
He runs his hands under the tap
to wash away the static.

Waterproof plasters peel off kneecaps in the shower
he squeezes them between his fingers and thumb
drops onto the sweating tiles outside
passes the soap between his hands
meditating over skin.

Water drips off elbows and hipbones
that never quite fleshed out.
Purple lotuses sliding across his ribcage
stretch
fifth position
arms above head
bloom.

Two-mile-away girl
in an apartment block
with walnut skin
black braids
sits in a bathtub
dips a cup in the water

pours it onto crop circles on her head
and her lips
candy purple
still smiling.

August

Red plastic line sagging in the middle
heavy with a full wash
clipped up with pink, lime green and blue pegs
swaying in the rolling wind.

The clouds gather overhead.

The hedges are overgrown
and our rented ladder wasn't tall enough to reach
so we wait
hoping it'll be easier to cut in Autumn.

Two golden dogs next door
make wagging panting circles behind the chain-link fence
kept safe
from clamping orange machines remaking the yard
balancing felled trunks precariously in digger mouths.

Men walking around in hard hats
and fluorescent orange vests
pause to take their thick gloves off
and stroke the dogs through the bars
whenever they walk past.

When they finish up for the day
they unlock the door.

The dogs run out and reclaim the garden.

On the grass
there is a rectangle of yellow light
cast from our kitchen.
We spice the potatoes
make steaming tea in a saucepan.

I wrap my arms around your waist
my head resting on your back
while you wash up the heavy pans.

We forget about the clothes on the line
remembering only after the grey clouds cluster
fill up
split open
cover the garden
completely.

It was one of the best days.

The thick wet jumpers
sprinting dogs
the scattered kitchen light.

Hope is Like Being Haunted

You move into a broken house
with layers of greasy dust
on every rickety surface
whistly windows painted shut
a basement that somebody was found under
in the 70s
and you expect things to go south.

But in the middle of the night
with the cold sheets pulled up to your nose
eyes open

there they are.

Spectres of hope
in half-stocked kitchen cupboards
through bathroom pipes
and behind mirrors.

Hope showing up between mouldy walls
sometimes solid and clear and singing
othertimes quiet and small and watching.

And when you feel the dark pull of the plughole
they are there to switch a light on
to rustle a cutlery drawer
to drop a picture frame into your lap
reminding you that you are not alone.

And even after you move out
if you choose to leave
they follow as they always have done
these faithful, hopeful ghosts
hovering over your retreating back
curling around the exhaust fumes
already belted into the passenger seat.

Blessing

Under the baptism of your bowed head
your warm hands and gentle eyes

you, my love, are a call to worship
a song on my first day of being born again

and I am open
to every ritual
of being loved
completely.

Four:
Fragments: Stories from the Other Side

Silverware

This evening, the forks and spoons have disappeared.

The drawers felt lighter
when we rolled them open.

So light it seemed to be ringing
high and clear
like a row of glass bells
that at first went unnoticed
then grew into a siren.

The only cutlery left are knives
butter knives and serrated edges
all the knives with mismatched handles
flowers
paisley
stainless steel
collected over a decade of moving houses
when our rent became too steep
when our street's water was shut off for good
when our children
were taken.

It is a message
to arm ourselves.

The chairs are gone
and there's nowhere to sit

so we stand with our knives
on the worn-down carpet
listening to our neighbours
shuffling behind their walls
opening their kitchen drawers too

and wait for the next steps
in a circle
around the dinner table

that has also gone missing.

There's No Time Like the Pandemic

Like quicksand
you sink less if you're absolutely still
but the fitness videos said the opposite
so we half-danced under soil
waiting to unshell.

Deer Watching

Tall tree-branch antlers
coiled sinews
amber eyes like flint rocks struck beneath cold hands

my palms prickle on the steering wheel
the car hood clicks in the unexpected stop

thinning pale arms of birch halo him
gold foil of leaves sift down
landing near silent hooves

his muscles contract under red-brown fur
he clips across white road markings

not breaking eye contact until the other side
head fixing towards the swallowing woods
thick underbrush parting for his body

he kicks off into the forest
splattering ribbons of mud and brittle leaves behind him

I almost bite my tongue in two
watch the shimmering space where he was
listen until my heart is the only thing left
still galloping.

Migration

There is salt and sea
and thirsty throats
and so many hands that hold on.

Fifty people on an orange lifeboat
designed for ten
blown up with panicked breaths
in half the time
only some of them have life vests
as if they don't all deserve to survive.

The water is both freedom and final
a possibility body
a rougher conveyer belt
that doesn't question your luggage or empty papers
but has no idea where you'll end up either
sending you off
with wild indifference.

The lifeboat rushes
with the desperate hope of better places
where the grass is quietly green
not filled with bullet cartridges
or bent knees forced apart like open staplers
but a slip
under the icy waters
can pull you onto another path.

But parts of you are left behind.

Gaps where people used to be
like mouthfuls of missing teeth.

Someone white-knuckled on the bottom of a truck
only half their body
arrived at their destination
still holding on.

These houses are uprooted
naked and shivering
you can sometimes see terrified eyes
trapped between the floorboards
waiting for the drop
wondering
if this
will be it.

Hands up
in the heavens praying
make this boat a shrine
a vessel
for holy cargo
make this boat documented and written
like scripture
a slow offering.

If everyone is still
and steady
hopefully
they will pass safely
over the ocean's open mouth.

Hold your breath until they get here.
Open borders like floodgates
          like mercy.

When they arrive
rush out to meet them
make sure those hands
have something steady to hold.

Union

We married with coins over our eyes
and a red veil over our heads
to shield us from early death
or buy our way back to each other if necessary.

Our matching shifts were blue and white brocade
and stitched neatly into the hem
our ancestors' teeth
gifted for good luck.

Grandmother walked in procession
carried a quarter of the heavy cloth
her thick gold rings knotted on brown paper hands.
She'd been bench-pressing bundles of scarves
for three months in preparation.

Grandfather cradled pink blessings
of garlands, threaded on white string.
Throughout the day he would place more garlands
around his neck
until his body receded
and he became a mountain of flowers.

Our parents covered the wedding urn in a white tea-towel
cracked it underfoot
then mended it together
filled the chasms with silver.

We could only marry when they'd finished.

But they'd been practicing for weeks
becoming efficient and artful
without losing spontaneity.
Our mothers delegated well.
Your father sorted the blood from the pottery
mine melted his necklace.

With a newly repaired urn by our side
finally, you held six arrowheads between your lips
I used the shafts to make a fire.

We threw in our sticks of cinnamon
the spices becoming infused in the veil
honey, smoke, constancy

to be shared later
with our mouths

the silver coins cooling
on the bedside table

just in case we should need them.

Sand Timer

brown sugar falling
like expectations

and I wonder if I cut the glass
in half
stir it into my tea
would I taste the last two minutes

and these words
and the impulse of breaking things

will it make me wise
will I feel all-knowing

like God
when he looks down
at people
divining fortune out of tea leaves
and it makes
him laugh

You Tell Me You're an Organ Donor

So when you die, your body will be claimed
by other people.

Should I find the saved
the chameleon ex-patient
and become friends with them
so I can feel your heart working somewhere else?

Will their kidneys have your memories?
The trips to the seaside
but always stopping at the first service station bathroom
for one last pee?
Will their cathedral lungs catch and hold a breath
when they see a buzzard or a dragonfly?
Will their blood be reheated?
Will their liver be clean too?
Will they celebrate with a small glass of champagne
for more days added onto the end of their life?

This is if your organs are well enough.
I'm sure they will be.
The meditation and slow living
will have kept them dishwasher-clean.

The kind of dishes that end up
packed into a cardboard box
donated to charity
displayed in that glass cabinet under the counter
the one they save for precious jewellery.

I'd sit beside them in the car on their journey
hold them one last time before they are given out separately

the heat from my hands long gone

ready for somebody else to warm.

'Upholding the Law Fairly and Firmly'
- Police Vision: 2025

blue uniform sirens
only protect their own

prey on dark skin
unholster fatality

nothing to stop them
holding down the weight of their law
firmly

La Vie En Rose

After a day of interacting with people
with their subtleties
and shifting eyes
and sighing
like an awkward Morse code
of what they wanted to do
and who they wanted to touch

he spent hours
pouring over the smallest gesture
pressing them with the weight of Bibles
the man at the bus stop
with mercury in his eyes
the florist with blooms in the corners of her mouth
as she handed him his change.

But they became curled between pages of scripture
unruly
they grew in their intricacies
and after a while
he stopped trying to translate.

Instead
letting this storm of unrequited gestures
wash over him like rain
never quite being able to hold on
the cold settling on his skin.

When he was younger
he'd become used to the sight
of women walking out the door
and he was the type of man
who never learnt how to unpack in other people's houses.

He found clarity in music.
It was his food
his pulse
his daily prayer.

It was like shrugging off his heavy coat
and finally being home.

The great jazz legends of history
told of love better than he ever could
so he put his body in their hands
and let them educate.

He learnt fidelity from Fats Waller
and how to play piano with a gun to your back
to a room full of gangsters.

He learnt hypnotism from Nina Simone
and how to make someone's whole body erupt
in goosebumps.

From Chet Baker he learnt people were not perfect
the ones you end up with are always a little funny.

He learnt how to play with a broken jaw
under a moon as blue as the way Art Tatum painted it.

He learnt the complexities of being human
a thousand messy emotions
without trying to pin them down and label them
like butterflies under glass
but they were there
in the grooves of the records he held
in the notes of their music
in the safety of his walls.

Life outside buzzed on
a hive of frustrated people
who huffed and stormed
when he walked slow.

Over time he settled
and was never happier
than when he was picking through his records
running his fingers across their slim covers
precious as books.

He grew amongst the reeds
in the belly of a saxophone
with the mouth of a trumpet
and teeth like piano keys
trombones under his skin
with the spine of a guitar string
and a chest like a drum.

He turned up the volume
and let the walls be coated
in song.

Transformation

When I've finished this life
folded my list back into my pocket
    comfortable with the unticked boxes
said some form of goodbye
held hands for the final time

    cremate me

    scatter me in the dark blue sea

there is peace there
    wild freedom in equal measure

                    parts of me
    will go further than others
    but that's okay

they'll be there for the long haul
greeting silver murmurations of fish and curling seaweed

joining the grains of sand turning over on their seabed
saying

    hey, I've got time
    and you're not confined to your hourglass yet

or sitting on the belly of a whale
    can I be a barnacle?
    I'll hitchhike on you
    let you know about all the sunsets I see

or maybe I'll end up as a message in a bottle
    feel all the hope rolled up inside
    remember how it felt to have all
    that desperate energy

maybe   float

    my grey form mixed with all that blue

    not having   to be anything   at all

I could
    dissolve
        eventually

    and
        always   taste

    like

        the

            sweetness

    of

            oceans

Five:
How to Turn Your Body into a Forest Fire

Regenerating

They say that every seven to ten years
skin cells completely regenerate.

Every ten years you have a new clean skeleton.
Every two to four weeks your epidermis has flaked off
and grown back.

So no matter what he touched, it no longer exists.

But there are times when you can still feel his hands.

Whilst bad memories are mostly quietened
unbidden they rise suddenly
like red flares in the dark.

You remember that half your heart stays with you
from the day it's first shaped to the moment it stops.

The lens of your eye remains too
for better or worse
never being able to unsee.

It is hard to sit with yourself.

But after ten years we know what to do.
Instead of suffocating the flames
we sit with our fresh bones against the radiator ribs
holding the blaze in our new hands

and we listen to each crackle.

We help it to stabilise
wait for it to calm.

It burns less
the longer you hold it.

Women of the Sea

Rise up
you are stronger than you believe
you have saltwater in your body
waves in your hips
your hair
your heartbeat.

The curves of your stomach roll up
like jellyfish
and you
have a killer sting.

You flow in unison
wash away the blood
purify
keep the things that shine
like sets of keys
promise rings slipped from loose fingers
a string of pearls
desperate to find its way back to the ocean

people too

pretty sailors
one look at you
and their eyes splinter like a shipwreck
the wood breaking
the ropes fraying
unsettling
in the soft parts of their bodies.

You
wash
their
lungs
clean.

And the ones who survive
have half-closed throats
clouded faces
and breaths that always seem
to hitch.

Because like the sea
you are softness and strength
freedom and life and utterly deadly
holy and blessed and terrifying.
You command the tides
every drop
the ebb and flow
and whether or not
to float or flood

it's all on you.

Poetry of Resistance
After Haki R. Madhubuti

The poetry of resistance
is written on placards
in the marches of *me too*
we are the ones we have been waiting for
and *silent no longer.*

It is passed on the lips of underground battles
from street corner preachers
to the boy-on-boy love of *yes.*
It is shouted at crowds by young women with shaved heads
we are worth more than your bullets.

It is whispered into the hollows of baby chests
as they are lowered into incubators
the prayers of first-time parents
willing them to survive
with their soft fingers
strong enough to cling to washing lines
even they have the tendency to hold on.

It is in the hands of a boy
who can't read words on pages.
They dance in his eyes
so he puts them on a scale and turns them into music.

It is two people who have never met
consoling each other in biro on public toilet walls
I feel so lonely
I feel the same way.

It's friends holding hands in the early hours saying
you will live through this.

It's a girl looking in bathroom mirrors
commanding
OVERCOME.

The poetry of resistance
is not ironed neatly onto pretty paper.
It is passed down generations
> memorised
>> like songs of your homeland.

It is a live thing
that refuses to be pressed between hardback.
It is loud and angry and fists and stay with me.

It is keep standing
> keep sitting
>> keep marching until they finally notice us
>> notice black bodies under blue sirens
>> it is not supposed to be that way.

It is radical self-love of bodies
that were never made to fit in hope chests
but who love exactly as they are.

It is be kind
> this will pass
> we can change things
> we believe we can
> one moment at a time.

It is survivors
brimming with purpose
with poetry in their skin.

It is protest
              it is in our bones to resist.

Know your voice is powerful
                          with the tendency to soar

keep it that way

    shout it from tower blocks

    we are electric thunderstorms in August

    the first calm breaths after a bad night

    when the sun finally comes up for air.

Art Lessons

Step into your Hermes-swift work boots
the burgundy brogues
with thick laces and chunky heels

throw back your sandalwood hair
thread on your wedding bangles
when you took yourself and said *I do*

you patron saint of carrying-on
you pilot light

rubbing a paste of haldi and rich volcanic soil
into your skin
glowing like Gaia
with Shiva thighs
and Kali-red tongue
unfurled on a conquered battlefield
wearing a necklace of the heads of crawling men

keep dancing on their backs
until they are palettes
ground into the dust

then you can add water

paint with them.

Rani Lakshmibai of Jhansi

They can erase us but they cannot bend us.

Little Manikarnika Tambe
was home schooled
in not only languages and arts
but fencing, shooting, and horsemanship.

In 1842 she married Maharaja Gangadhar Rao Newalkar.
With sindoor fresh on her hairline
chura glittering on her wrists
she stepped into her new name
Lakshmibai
Queen of Jhansi.

Not intending to give up her education,
before breakfast
she would weightlift, wrestle and steeplechase
her red salwar rippling behind her as she flew on her horse
clearing fences and ditches
her laughter filling up the courtyard
through each of the palace's embroidered rooms.

In 1851 she birthed a son
a delicate fleeting boy
his skin glowing softly
his curling tiny fingers.

And at four months old
when his light dwindled
and then
extinguished
his father, the Maharaja
died of heartbreak.

When the British came
to claim her land
she did not throw herself
onto the funeral pyre.

She became the flames.

Rani Lakshmibai of Jhansi
swapped the jewels she wore for armour
and a voice that could crush mountains
a white shankha in her throat
ready for war.

With her adopted son as her chosen heir
she refused to surrender
or be gentle.

And there was solidarity
like Jhalkharibai
skilled in swordplay and artistry
she looked just like Lakshmi
a double
she used this as a trick
to help her queen escape
didn't care about the danger.

They led the Durga Dal
a fierce group of female warriors
devastatingly dangerous.
Durgas
protective like the Mother Goddess
with weapons and armour
over soft brown skin.

In Gwalior, June 1858
in her final battle
avenging the 5000 brown bodies
of the brutally massacred
Rani Lakshmibai rode with a sword in her hand
and her child strapped to her back.

When she fell on the battlefield
her armour filling with blood
she refused to let her body be taken by British hands
even in death.

And as Queen Lakshmibai lay dying
under a tamarind tree
she watched the sunset and ignited.

These were great women
buried by history
women who fought their trauma
with enough blood to drown their enemies in.

Let us unforget their fierceness
these mothers
and widows
and daughters
who rose up and fought for freedom.

They can erase us but they cannot bend us.

Remember that
when you are made to feel small or weak
step in to that tiger skin
and fight back.

FIGHT BACK with words
FIGHT BACK with action or
FIGHT BACK by living the best life you possibly can.

You are woman.
You bleed for over half a century
you are made of pain stitched together
you are forced upon
you are interrupted and silenced
you were not given a licence to your own body
that is kept in the hands of
old white men
but we can take it back.

Use your power
it is here
resist
survive
be soft
be fierce
be the tiger
be the flame
be the whole forest fire too.

Sometimes you might have to bend
but with roots like these
you will never
ever
break.

Body

1.

As a child you learn your squishy form
that rolls giggling with you down the hill at lunchtime
    collecting grass in your plait
carrying you breathless across the sports day finish line
    taking home the rush

never able to stay within the lines
                                    wiggling constantly

you use every muscle gifted to you
    jumping from monkey bars to playground floor
    sliding
    see-saw
    shouting down monsters behind basement doors

sometimes losing pieces of your body along the way

thinner knees after rounders
    from over-diving to safety

a milk tooth lost in the woodchips
    wrapped in a tissue

but finding your body has your back

new thick skin within a week
and no scabs needed

growing stronger teeth in the same gaps

and you still smile wide in pictures while they grow back
    dreaming you'll be able to devour
    a whole corn on the cob
    suck on a blueberry gumball until it's gone.

2.

Growing up
some of us are taken.

Bodies rolled under
somebody else's sofa
glass marbles
    dull
    cracked
    separated.

It takes a while
to crawl back out.

3.

You are still the body you grew up with.

The sweat of always trying
    of softening jaws
    and unclenching stomachs.

Even so
you have bad days

hold your body tighter
        when you feel like letting go

and in the quiet
stretch up arms
in glory.

Feel the temple you are built in
        the light you are growing
        in parts you didn't know existed.

Tip your head back and keep letting the light in
        let the column of your throat drink it
        like pillars for holy buildings

your palms are open
and you are full.

Worship your body like the gift it is
        in every form it goes through

this arrangement of tiny miracles
this anthem of resilience.

Prayers are written in your skin like braille.

You can always find yourself
even in the dark.

GLOSSARY

Arbi: A root vegetable most commonly known as taro.

Atta: Wholemeal wheat flour used to make flatbreads such as naan, roti and chapatti.

Bhangra: Traditional folk dance and music from Punjab.

Cha/Chai: A rich, hot drink made with black tea, milk, sugar, and various spices such as cloves, cardamom, ginger, cinnamon, fennel, star anise and black peppercorns.

Chapatti: Unleavened flatbread, roti.

Chunni: A scarf worn usually by Indian women.

Chura: A set of bangles traditionally worn by a bride on her wedding day and for a period after, especially in Punjabi weddings.

Durga: A goddess created by Brahma, Vishnu, Shiva and the lesser gods to slay the demon Mahishasura. Embodying their collective energy, essence and the true source of their inner power, Durga is more powerful than them all. She is often depicted riding a lion (sometimes depicted as a tiger), and holding a special weapon of a different god in each of her eight to ten arms.

Gurdwaras: The place of worship for Sikhs. Gurdwara means 'doorway to the Guru' in Punjabi.

Haldi: Turmeric, a yellow spice powder.

Jalebi: A spiral-shaped crisp & juicy sweet made with all-purpose flour, gram flour and sugar syrup.

Kali: (Sanskrit: 'She Who Is Black' or 'She Who Is Death') Hindu goddess of death, time and change. She is also worshipped as the great protector and mother goddess. Kali has fierce eyes, fangs and a lolling tongue. She wears a garland of human heads and a skirt of human arms, and is often shown wearing a tiger skin.

Maharaja: An Indian ruler/king.

Mandir: Hindu temple/place of worship.

Manjas: Woven rope bed common in India.

Methi: Fenugreek, a herb.

Parvati: The goddess of power, nourishment, harmony, devotion, and motherhood. She is the consort of Shiva and mother of Ganesh and Kartikeya. Parvati is depicted as peaceful and beautiful in a red sari and has either two or four arms. Her anger causes great destruction.

Rani: An Indian queen. The name Rani means 'she is singing', and 'joyous song'.

Roti: Unleavened flatbread, chapatti.

Rupees: Money used in India, Pakistan, Sri Lanka, Nepal, Mauritius, and Seychelles.

Sari: A traditional Indian dress consisting of a single length of cotton or silk. Usually intricately patterned and/or brightly coloured.

Salwar/Salwar Kameez: Traditional Indian suit. It consists of a long tunic worn over pyjama-like trousers that are loose and pleated.

Shankha: A conch shell. The shankha is a sacred emblem of Vishnu and was blown during important events, celebrations, religious rituals, and by Krishna at the start and end of war.

Shiva: (Sanskrit: 'Auspicious One') God of destruction, time and arts. The Destroyer of Evil; God of Yoga and Meditation. One of the three main Hindu gods with Brahma and Vishnu.

Sindoor: A traditional vermillion powder from India. Usually worn by married women along their hair parting.

ACKNOWLEDGEMENTS

Thank you to my wonderful family for everything you do. It's thanks to you that I exist - I love you all very much. Thank you Mum, Dad, Suman and Jagdeep. Thank you as well to the rest of my incredible extended family.

Thank you to my talented, kind husband Adrian Saredia-Brayley for illustrating the front cover, and for all his endless support throughout this book (and life!). His Instagram is @_witchesgetstitches_ if you want to see more of his beautiful art.

Thank you to lovely Helen 'Helbo' Seymour, the Super Fun Best Egg. You know what you've done. (Not a threat.)

Thank you to Brigitte Aphrodite and Gaz AKA Quiet Boy for your beautiful, constant support and friendship, and to Angela for your generosity and eggs, and little Sappho for all the smiles and ra-ras. I am so blessed to have found you all.

Thank you to Lisa Mead and everyone at Apples and Snakes for your time, kindness, guidance, opportunities and all your support.

Thank you to Anne, John, Janice, Alec, Natalie and all the lovely staff at EBP Kent for your support and encouragement.

Thank you to Jacob Sam-La Rose, Malika Booker, Joelle Taylor and Kat Francois for your brilliant mentoring.

Thank you to all you beautiful poets in Canterbury for your love, support and opportunities from day one.

Huge thank you to Stuart Bartholomew and all those at Verve for being patient, for having faith in me and for publishing my first collection.

And finally, thank *you*, for reading this book. You are wonderful and I appreciate you so much.

ABOUT VERVE POETRY PRESS

Verve Poetry Press is an award-winning press that focused initially on meeting a local need in Birmingham - a need for the vibrant poetry scene here in Brum to find a way to present itself to the poetry world via publication. Co-founded by Stuart Bartholomew and Amerah Saleh, it now publishes poets from all corners of the UK and beyond - poets that speak to the city's varied and energetic qualities and will contribute to its many poetic stories.

As well as publishing full poetry collections, we have a colourful pamphlet series, many featuring poets who have performed at our sister festival - and a poetry show series which captures the magic of longer poetry performance pieces by festival alumni such as Polarbear, Matt Abbott and Imogen Stirling.

The press has been voted Most Innovative Publisher at the Saboteur Awards, and has won the Publisher's Award for Poetry Pamphlets at the Michael Marks Awards.

Like the festival, we strive to think about poetry in inclusive ways and embrace the multiplicity of approaches towards this glorious art.

www.vervepoetrypress.com
@VervePoetryPres
mail@vervepoetrypress.com